RUTH BADER GINSBURG

RUTH BADER GINSBURG

ICONIC SUPREME COURT JUSTICE

JAMES ROLAND

LERNER PUBLICATIONS ◆ MINNEAPOLIS

For my mother, Janette, an inspiration to all who know and love her

Lerner Publications Company
A division of Lerner Publishing Group, Inc.
241 First Avenue North
Minneapolis, MN USA 55401

For reading levels and more information, look up this title at www.lernerbooks.com.

The images in this book are used with the permission of: AP Photo/Cliff Owen, p. 2; AP Photo/ Doug Mills, pp. 6, 31; Collection of the Supreme Court of the United States, pp. 8 (photo by Richard Strauss, Smithsonian Institution), 9, 11, 14, 15, 19, 22, 24, 25, 41 (photo by Steve Petteway); AP Photo/Anthony Camerano, p. 10; Eustress/Wikimedia Commons (CC BY-SA 3.0), p. 13; © Kim Karpeles/Alamy, p. 16; © H Armstrong Roberts/ClassicStock/Alamy, p. 17; © Bettmann/Corbis, pp. 18, 23; © BrOnXbOmBr21/Wikimedia Commons (CC BY 2.5), p. 20; © Brooks Kraft/Corbis, p. 26; © David Hume Kennerly/Getty Images, p. 27; © Fanny Carrier/AFP/ Getty Images, p. 32; AP Photo/Marcy Nighswander, p. 28; © Jim Bourg/Reuters/Corbis, p. 33; AP Photo/Stephen R. Brown, p. 35; Rex USA, p. 36; AP Photo/Stephan Savoia, p. 38; © Pete Marovich/EPA/Alamy, p. 39; © Dana Edelson/NBC/NBCU Photo Bank via Getty Images, p. 40.

Cover: Collection of the Supreme Court of the United States, photo by Steve Petteway

Main body text set in Rotis Serif Std 55 Regular 13.5/17. Typeface provided by Adobe Systems.

Library of Congress Cataloging-in-Publication Data

Roland, James, author.
   Ruth Bader Ginsburg : iconic Supreme Court justice / James Roland.
     pages cm
   Includes bibliographical references and index.
   ISBN 978-1-5124-0596-5 (lb : alk. paper) — ISBN 978-1-5124-0597-2 (eb pdf)
     1. Ginsburg, Ruth Bader—Juvenile literature. 2. Judges—United States—Biography—Juvenile literature. 3. United States. Supreme Court—Biography—Juvenile literature. 4. Women judges—United States—Biography—Juvenile literature. 5. Law—United States—Juvenile literature. I. Title.
   KF8745.G56R65 2016
   347.73′2634—dc23 [B]   2015025410

Manufactured in the United States of America
1 – CG – 12/31/15

CONTENTS

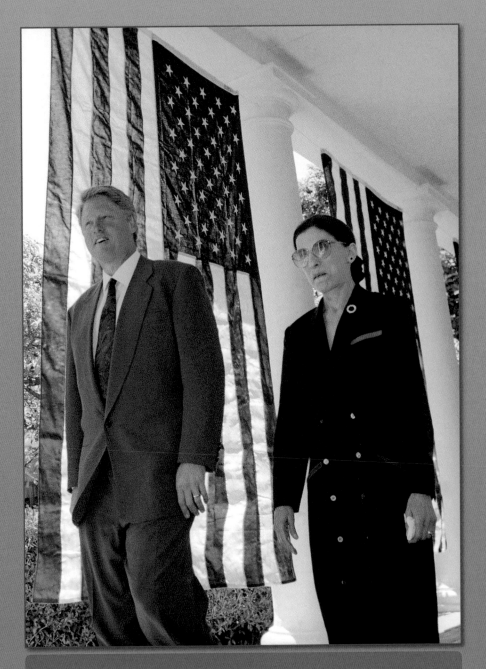

Ruth Bader Ginsburg walks with President Bill Clinton toward the White House Rose Garden on June 14, 1993.

On a sunny Sunday afternoon in June 1993, Ruth Bader Ginsburg stood quietly in the White House Rose Garden next to President Bill Clinton. He had asked Ginsburg only a day earlier if she would be willing to take the place of Justice Byron White, who was retiring from the US Supreme Court.

Ginsburg was excited about the opportunity. She would be just the second woman ever to serve on the Supreme Court. The first, Justice Sandra Day O'Connor, had been on the nation's highest court since 1981.

During the Rose Garden ceremony introducing his selection to the public and the press, Clinton praised Ginsburg's distinguished career as a lawyer and then a judge. "Over the course of a lifetime, in her pioneering work on behalf of the women of this country, she has compiled a truly historic record of achievement in the finest traditions of American law and citizenship," he said.

When it was her turn to publicly accept the nomination, Ginsburg thanked Clinton and many others, including her husband, Martin. But she saved her last thank-you for her late mother. "I pray that I may be all that she would have been had she lived in an age when women could aspire and achieve, and daughters are cherished as much as sons," she said, as the president and others in attendance choked back tears.

Ruth's mother, Celia Amster Bader, never attended college. Instead, she worked to help her family pay for her brother to get a college education. This was very common when she was young. Most women were not encouraged

In 1993, Ginsburg *(back right)* became the second woman to serve on the Supreme Court. The first woman was Sandra Day O'Connor *(front left)*.

to pursue college, let alone a career in law. But Celia Bader wanted her daughter to have more freedom and choices than she'd had.

And even though she had died the day before Ruth graduated from high school, Celia Bader had set her daughter on a path that would make her an iconic figure in the American legal system and a role model for women and men alike.

KIKI

Ruth Bader was the second daughter of Celia and Nathan Bader. Her older sister, Marilyn, died of meningitis when Ruth was very young. Ruth, who was born in 1933, never had any other siblings. Nicknamed Kiki (pronounced "kicky") by her sister, Ruth was raised in the Flatbush area of Brooklyn, New York. Her father sold clothing, and her mother was a homemaker.

Ruth went by the family nickname Kiki while growing up in the 1930s.

Ruth grew up in the Flatbush area of Brooklyn, New York.

Ruth and her mother often visited the local library, fueling the future Supreme Court justice's passion for reading and knowledge. "One of my greatest pleasures as a child was sitting on my mother's lap when she would read to me, and then going to the library with her," Ruth said. "In fact, she deposited me in the children's section of the library and went to get her hair done. By the time she'd come back, I had the five books that I would take home for that week."

As an eighth grader, Ruth edited her school's student newspaper, called the *Highway Herald*. She once wrote an editorial about some of the most important documents in history, including the Declaration of Independence and the United Nations charter. She was later part of her high school honor society.

Ruth had a lighter side too. She twirled the baton and was on her high school's pep squad, called the Go-Getters. As a member of the Go-Getters, she wore a black satin jacket, sold tickets to football games, and helped promote her school's sports teams in other ways. Ruth also loved music and played cello in the school orchestra. During the summers, Ruth attended Camp Che-Na-Wah, a Jewish summer camp in upstate New York. When she turned thirteen, she served as the "camp rabbi," leading services for her fellow campers.

Before she had even reached her teen years, though, Ruth learned about discrimination against Jewish people. She and her family paid close attention to the Nazi persecution of Jews in Europe before and during World War II (1939–1945).

Ruth leads campers in prayer at Camp Che-Na-Wah in Minerva, New York, in 1948.

Even at home in the United States, life was sometimes difficult for Jewish families. During one family trip in Pennsylvania, the Baders drove by a hotel sign that said, "No dogs or Jews allowed."

She would endure different types of discrimination later in life, especially as a woman in a field traditionally dominated by men. But these experiences helped shape Ruth's desire to help fight discrimination for the rest of her life.

BALANCING EDUCATION AND A FAMILY

In 1950 Ruth's mother died after a long battle with cancer. It was the day before Ruth was to graduate from Brooklyn's James Madison High School, a public school that now includes a mock courtroom in its legal studies program named after the Supreme Court justice. Losing her mother was heartbreaking for Ruth. But she knew the best way to honor her mom's memory was to make the most of her education and career.

"My mother told me two things constantly," Ginsburg recalled. "One was to be a lady, and the other was to be independent." And so, this independent young lady left Brooklyn for Cornell University in Ithaca, New York, determined to one day become a lawyer.

At Cornell she helped one of her professors with research on blacklists in the entertainment industry. In the United States in the 1950s, a blacklist was a list of

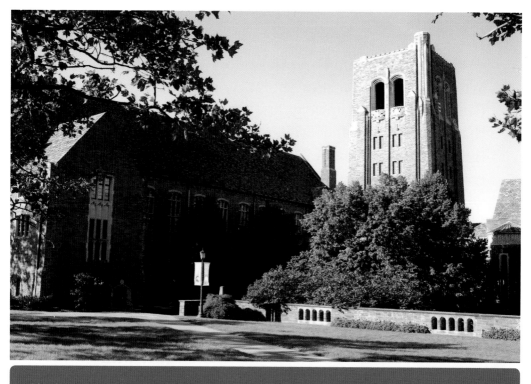

Ginsburg studied law and government at Cornell University in Ithaca, New York, in the 1950s.

people suspected of being Communists. People on these lists were sometimes fired from their jobs or were barred from getting work elsewhere. It didn't matter whether the person was truly a Communist or not. Once he or she was accused, that person's life was never the same.

Ginsburg saw many attorneys risk their careers by defending blacklisted entertainers, college professors, and other individuals in court and before Congress. It wouldn't be long before Ginsburg would be in court representing other people being treated unfairly. First, though, she would need to complete her schooling.

Ginsburg graduated with honors with a bachelor of arts in government. But the university was important to Ginsburg in another very lasting way. It was at Cornell that she met a prelaw student named Martin Ginsburg. He was a year ahead of Ruth in school. The two were college sweethearts who continued their courtship while Ruth finished her last year at Cornell and Martin started at Harvard Law School in Cambridge, Massachusetts.

They got married in June 1954, the same month Ruth graduated at the top of her class from Cornell. But instead of going back to Massachusetts with Martin, Ruth found

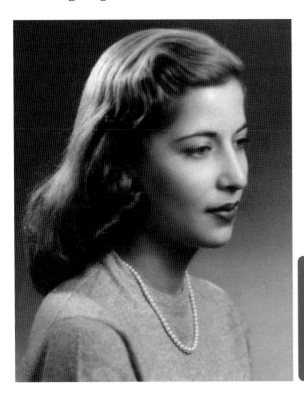

herself in Fort Sill, Oklahoma. Martin had been a US Army Reserve officer, and after Ruth's graduation, he was called up for active duty. In 1955 the couple had their first child, a daughter they named Jane.

This portrait of Ginsburg was taken in December 1953, during her senior year at Cornell.

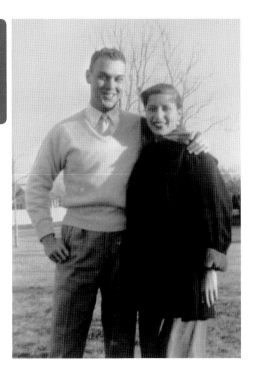

Martin and Ruth were college sweethearts at Cornell. They were married on June 23, 1954.

After Martin's army duty ended, he returned to Harvard. Ruth also enrolled at Harvard Law School, but she wasn't able to focus entirely on her studies. She had to take care of baby Jane as well as Martin, who underwent surgery and treatment for testicular cancer the following year. But Ruth somehow managed to take care of everyone and everything at home while also becoming one of Harvard's top law students.

Ruth Bader Ginsburg's experience at Harvard was difficult, though, and not just because of the demanding courses and the responsibilities at home. Women had been allowed to attend Harvard Law only since 1950. There were just nine women in Ginsburg's class out of about five hundred first-year law students. The female students weren't given much respect. The dean even asked the women how they felt about taking away spots from qualified men.

Law students at Harvard face difficult classes and homework, but the program is known for producing some of the best lawyers in the world.

But Ginsburg persevered. She became the first woman on the *Harvard Law Review*. A law review is a journal with articles about court cases and other law-related subjects. The journal is published by the best students at a particular law school. Ginsburg enjoyed writing. She later became one of the more prolific opinion writers on the Supreme Court. A court opinion is a summary of the case and an explanation of why the court ruled the way it did. But that was still many years away.

Despite her early academic success at Harvard, Ginsburg wouldn't get her degree there. Another big move was about to send her life in a new direction.

THE STRUGGLE TO FIND A JOB

Martin Ginsburg had been offered a great job with a big law firm in New York City right after he graduated. The couple wanted to keep the family together in one place. Even though she was just a year from graduating, Ruth Ginsburg left Harvard and transferred to Columbia Law School in New York. Both universities are part of a small group of schools that make up the prestigious Ivy League.

She soon earned a place on the *Columbia Law Review*, becoming the first person ever to be part of the law reviews at both Harvard and Columbia. Ginsburg also graduated first in her class at Columbia. She faced less discrimination there compared with Harvard.

The Ginsburg family moved to New York City in 1958.

In spite of her glowing academic credentials, Ginsburg encountered some challenges in finding a job. Shortly after her Columbia graduation, Ginsburg was recommended by one of her professors to be a law clerk for Supreme Court justice Felix Frankfurter. Law clerks, sometimes called judicial clerks, help judges do research and write opinions on cases. It's a common entry-level position for new lawyers, and it helps recent graduates gain work experience within the legal profession.

But Frankfurter, who had been on the Supreme Court since 1939, rejected Ginsburg. He said he wasn't ready to hire a woman. Ginsburg wasn't offered a job by any major New York law firms either. As a woman and a mother, she faced a lot of discrimination. Ginsburg had worked for a summer for a large firm in New York. She had hoped that summer internship would turn into a job offer after graduation. Yet that offer never came.

Justice Felix Frankfurter served on the Supreme Court from January 1939 to August 1962.

Ginsburg and her husband play with their daughter, Jane, at home in New York in the summer of 1958.

But Ginsburg was not one to give up on her dreams. Several years after she started her term on the Supreme Court, Ginsburg told an interviewer that she could be grateful that she hadn't gotten the job with that New York law firm. She said sometimes in life a defeat can lead to a better opportunity later on.

"You think about what would have happened," Ginsburg said. "Suppose I had gotten a job as a permanent associate. Probably I would have climbed up the ladder and today I would be a retired partner. So often in life, things that you regard as an impediment turn out to be great good fortune."

Ginsburg finally got a job clerking for US district judge Edmund Palmieri in New York City, which she did for nearly two years. At the invitation of Columbia law professor Hans Smit, she left her clerk job to join

Columbia's Project on International Civil Procedure from 1961 to 1963. There she researched laws and legal procedures from other countries and proposed ways that the legal system in the United States might be improved. As part of her work, Ginsburg learned Swedish and worked in Sweden briefly, helping a Swedish judge write a law book. She was later given an honorary degree from the University of Lund in Sweden.

The Columbia Project experience had a profound effect on the way Ginsburg approached her work as

In 1961 Ginsburg returned to Columbia University to work on the college's Project on International Civil Procedure.

a judge and, later, as a Supreme Court justice. She often looked to international court cases to help her form opinions on the cases she heard. This philosophy has earned her some criticism from people who think US judges should only interpret US cases and the Constitution to reach their decisions.

Smit tried to convince Columbia Law School to make Ginsburg a professor when the project ended. When that didn't work out, Ruth took a job as a law professor at Rutgers University Law School in New Jersey.

FIGHTING FOR WOMEN'S RIGHTS

In 1965 the Ginsburgs had their second child, a son named James. Around the same time, Ginsburg started her longtime involvement with women's rights. The New Jersey office of the American Civil Liberties Union (ACLU) was receiving frequent complaints of discrimination against women. The ACLU fights for individual rights and liberties under the laws of the United States. Many of the women's rights cases being handled by the New Jersey ACLU office found their way to Ruth Bader Ginsburg at Rutgers.

The next several years would prove to be exciting ones, not just for Ginsburg but also for the women's movement. They were also very busy times. Ginsburg worked as both a law professor and an attorney helping the ACLU with many cases. One discrimination case

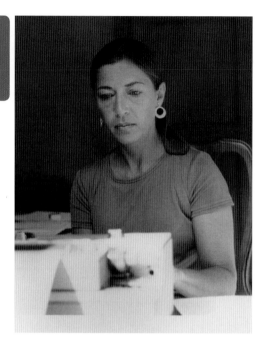

In the 1970s, Ginsburg argued cases to improve women's rights.

went all the way to the Supreme Court in 1971. The justices ruled in favor of Ginsburg's side. A year later, the ACLU created the Women's Rights Project. Ginsburg was named codirector. Also in 1972, Ginsburg accepted a job offer from Columbia Law School, making her the first tenured woman on its faculty. Tenured college professors cannot be fired unless the college proves that they did something wrong.

The 1970s saw many changes for women in the United States. A wider variety of careers were opening up to women, and the number of women graduating from college rose dramatically. But a lot of laws were unfair to women. And in many parts of the country, women were still fighting for equal treatment and equal opportunities.

In the middle of that fight was Ginsburg. She believed very strongly that men and women shouldn't be treated differently under the law. She bravely took on cases aimed at erasing those differences in state and national laws.

From 1973 to 1976, she argued six women's rights cases before the Supreme Court and won five of them. This work, along with other cases she took on in lower courts, helped women make great strides in achieving legal equality.

The first case she argued and won before the Supreme Court, *Frontiero v. Richardson*, took place in 1973. It involved a female air force lieutenant, Sharron Frontiero, and her husband, Joseph, who challenged a law that treated male and female military service members differently. Under the law, a man in the armed services could claim his wife as a legal dependent and qualify for an increased housing allowance, even if his wife did not depend on his income. But a married woman in the service had to prove that she provided her husband with more than half his financial support

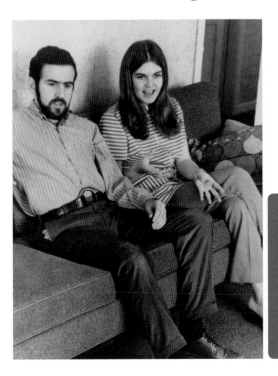

Lieutenant Sharron Frontiero *(right)* filed a lawsuit against the air force for gender discrimination. Ginsburg argued the Frontiero case before the Supreme Court in 1973.

for her to qualify for extra money to pay for their housing expenses. Ginsburg argued that such laws were prejudiced against women. She successfully proved that there was no reason for the law to treat men and women differently.

In another case, *Duren v. Missouri*, she argued that a Missouri law was unfair because it said that men had to sit on juries but that women had the option not to serve on jury duty. Ginsburg believed this law was basically saying that women weren't as important as men in the court system.

After spending most of the 1970s as an attorney arguing cases before judges, Ginsburg would spend the rest of her career listening and ruling on cases. But her role in the fight for women's rights and greater equality for everyone would only grow in the years ahead.

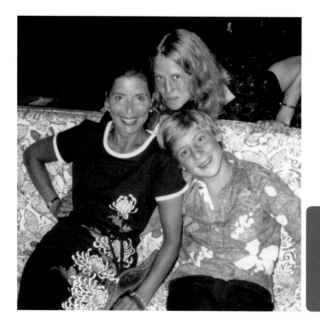

Ginsburg with her daughter, Jane, and son, James, in December 1979.

APPOINTED JUDGE AND JUSTICE

During the administration of President Jimmy Carter (1977–1981), there were no openings on the Supreme Court. But even though he couldn't place someone new on the Supreme Court, Carter did nominate many people as judges on federal courts around the nation. There are several types of federal courts. They hear cases involving the constitutionality of a law, disputes between states, international treaties, and other major issues. Federal courts have authority over state and local courts, though not as much power as the Supreme Court.

Carter made a special effort to nominate more women and minorities as judges in these important courts. In 1980, shortly before he lost his reelection bid to Ronald Reagan, Carter named Ruth Bader Ginsburg to the US Court of Appeals in Washington, DC. There are thirteen federal courts of appeals around the country. They are one step below the Supreme Court in our legal system.

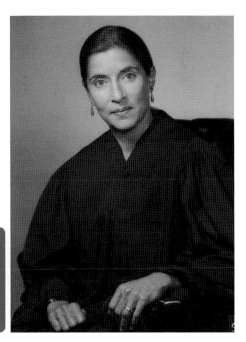

Ginsburg in her judicial robes during her first term on the US Court of Appeals in 1980

A court of appeals has a panel of three judges instead of a jury to decide each case. If someone loses in a US Court of Appeals, the next and final stop is the Supreme Court.

While on the US Court of Appeals in Washington, DC, Ginsburg wrote more than three hundred opinions. She also developed a reputation for building consensus among her fellow panel judges. Among the judges she served with was Antonin Scalia. Despite their contrasting political and judicial philosophies, Scalia and Ginsburg became friends. Scalia was appointed to the Supreme Court in 1986 and continued his friendly sparring with Ginsburg when she joined him seven years later.

By the time Scalia was named to the Supreme Court, there was already one woman justice. So the idea that

Ginsburg might one day make it to the Supreme Court wasn't too outrageous. In 1981 Reagan had selected Sandra Day O'Connor as the first female Supreme Court justice. Even though O'Connor was considered a conservative judge and Ginsburg a liberal judge, Ginsburg was thrilled

Antonin Scalia served with Ginsburg on both the US Court of Appeals and the Supreme Court. The two justices are close friends.

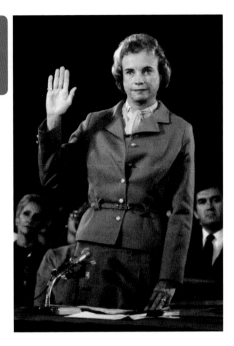

that a woman was finally part of the highest court in the nation.

"I thought it was terrific for the country," Ginsburg said later. "There was no chance that I was going to be nominated by President Reagan. But it was certainly time. I remember being in my car, turning on the radio, hearing the news, and thinking, 'Isn't this grand!'"

After O'Connor, the next four Supreme Court justices to be appointed were Scalia, Anthony Kennedy, David Souter, and Clarence Thomas. Then, in June 1993, only a few months after being sworn into office, Clinton made his first appointment to the high court. He named Ginsburg, making her the second female justice and the first Jewish female justice. The second Jewish woman to serve on the Supreme Court was Justice Elena Kagan. She was appointed by President Barack Obama in 2010, four years after Sandra Day O'Connor retired. The previous year, Obama had appointed Justice Sonia Sotomayor to the high court. For about two hundred years, no women had been on the Supreme Court. By the fall of 2010, three of the nine justices were women.

During her first week on the Supreme Court, Ginsburg wasted little time in establishing herself as an enthusiastic justice. She dove right into her first case, questioning the lawyers who were presenting it.

At a 2015 event at Harvard, retired Justice David Souter introduced Ginsburg by sharing his initial impression of her. Souter and Scalia were known to be aggressive questioners of attorneys during Supreme Court cases. But Ginsburg started firing off questions before anyone else could speak. Souter told the crowd at Harvard that Scalia whispered to him, "You and I may have asked

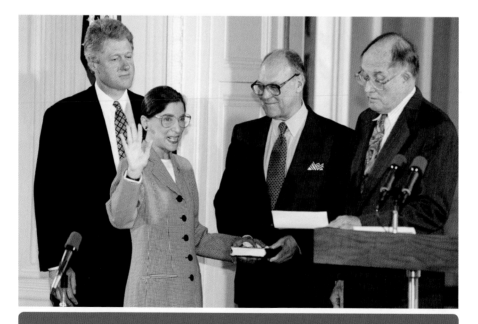

Ginsburg takes the oath of office on August 10, 1993, while her husband, Martin (center), looks on.

our last question in this courtroom." Souter also referred to Ginsburg as a "tiger justice."

ROLE IN THE SUPREME COURT

Though assertive in the courtroom, Ginsburg has a reputation for encouraging camaraderie among her fellow justices. She and Scalia often have very different opinions on cases and are frequently vocal in their disagreements. However, they have been good friends for many years. They have attended the opera together and have even vacationed together. Before Ginsburg's husband died in 2010, the Ginsburgs always had New Year's Eve dinner with Scalia and his wife, Maureen.

In a 2015 *Time* magazine article that named Ginsburg one of the 100 Most Influential People, Justice Scalia complimented his dear friend for her intelligence and her positive influence on the other eight justices. He wrote,

Having had the good fortune to serve beside her on both courts, I can attest that her opinions are always thoroughly considered, always carefully crafted, and almost always correct (which is to say we sometimes disagree). That much is apparent for all to see. What only her colleagues know is that her suggestions improve the opinions the rest of us write, and that she is a source of collegiality and good judgment in all our work.

THE SUPREME COURT

The Supreme Court is made up of nine judges called justices. When there is an opening on the court, the president nominates a judge. The US Senate must approve the nomination before the judge can be sworn in as a Supreme Court justice. Members of the Supreme Court are referred to as justices, to distinguish them from judges.

The cases that come before the Supreme Court usually have national importance and involve very serious subjects. These are cases that have been argued and appealed in lower courts. It is the Supreme Court's job to interpret the Constitution to help reach a decision. The Supreme Court can also decide whether federal, state, and even local governments are acting constitutionally. In addition, the Constitution gives the Supreme Court the power to decide whether the president is acting within the law.

In a case that comes before the Supreme Court, justices listen to lawyers representing both sides and ask questions to better understand the case. Justices meet by themselves, without an audience or the media present, to discuss the case. The justices also do a lot of reading. They study the background of the case they are hearing, as well as similar cases. The justices finally must vote on the case. Sometimes, it is a unanimous vote, 9–0. But it can often be a close 5–4 vote. The decisions are final and cannot be appealed. If the vote isn't unanimous, one justice writes the majority opinion and a justice in the minority writes what is called the dissenting opinion. These opinions are entered into the official record of the Supreme Court for the public to read.

Ginsburg also enjoyed a close relationship with Justice O'Connor, who retired from the Supreme Court in 2006. "She has been very much like a big sister," Ginsburg said of O'Connor. "I think we have an enormous affection and respect for each other, even though on some very important issues we are going to be on opposite sides."

On some cases, Ginsburg and O'Connor were very much in agreement. In 1996 Ginsburg and the other justices ruled on a case that in many ways summed up her longtime fight for equal rights for women. In *United States v. Virginia*, the Supreme Court ruled that the Virginia Military Institute (VMI) should have to admit women. For more than 150 years, VMI had trained men to become army officers. Ginsburg wrote in the majority decision that women should have the same opportunities as men, including the right to attend a public university such as VMI.

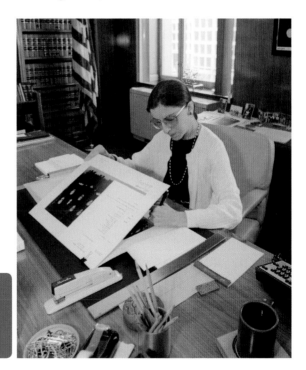

Ginsburg at work in her Washington, DC, office in 1993

In many cases, however, Ginsburg faced opposition from the majority of justices. In one well-known case, *Ledbetter v. Goodyear Tire & Rubber Co.*, Ginsburg was in the minority of a 5–4 vote. But even though the vote didn't go Ginsburg's way, the case eventually led to a change in federal law that benefited women in the workplace.

In the case, a Goodyear manager named Lilly Ledbetter complained that her salary was consistently less than male managers doing similar work, even though the men had the same amount of experience as Ledbetter or even less. The case was actually very complicated. The key issue involved the amount of time an employee has to file a charge of pay discrimination. Ledbetter hadn't made her complaint within the required 180 days of Goodyear's decision not to increase her salary. But her case would lead to a change in the way companies had to respond to such complaints. Two years after the case was decided, Obama signed into law the Lilly Ledbetter Fair Pay Act of 2009. It changed the way the 180-day rule is applied, making it easier for employees to challenge the fairness of their pay.

And in one of the most controversial cases to come before the Supreme Court during Ginsburg's time on the bench, she was also in the minority. The case was *Bush v. Gore*, and it determined the outcome of the 2000 presidential election. The case centered on a dispute between the candidates, Vice President Al Gore and Texas governor George W. Bush, about the vote totals and recount procedures in Florida. The justices voted 5–4 that the Florida Supreme Court had acted unconstitutionally in the way it ruled on the recount. The decision essentially sealed the victory for Bush.

Even though Ginsburg was in the minority, the case did underscore her belief that the Supreme Court should, at times, defer to other levels of government. In this famous case, she believed that the United States Supreme Court should not have overruled the Florida Supreme Court's

Al Gore *(left)* and George W. Bush were candidates for the 2000 presidential election. The votes were so close that some states, including Florida, had to recount their ballots to confirm an accurate tally.

decision in how a state law was being interpreted. She argued that the matter of recount deadlines and other procedures were the responsibility of Florida officials or perhaps Congress, and not the United States Supreme Court.

Every Supreme Court justice is in the majority or the minority at some point. Ginsburg once said that it does bother her when the votes don't go her way. But she doesn't stay down for long. "I'm dejected, but only momentarily, when I can't get the fifth vote for something I think is very important," she said. "But then you go on to the next challenge and you give it your all. You know that these important issues are not going to go away. They are going to come back again and again. There'll be another time, another day."

AWAY FROM COURT

Though being a judge is a time-consuming job, Ginsburg has always found time for her other interests. She still loves reading, especially mystery stories. Her favorite authors are Amanda Cross and Dorothy Sayers.

Ginsburg also loves music, especially opera. Her favorite composers include Verdi, Puccini, and Mozart. Because the Washington, DC, opera community knows about Ginsburg's love of opera, she was invited to be part of two productions in the nation's capital. In a Washington National Opera production of *Ariadne auf Naxos*, she was an extra wearing full makeup and a

Ginsburg *(center)* appeared in a production of the opera *Ariadne auf Naxos* in January 1994. Justice Scalia *(center right)* joined her in the performance.

powdered wig. She was joined onstage by fellow justice Scalia, also a big opera fan.

In another production, a famous lighthearted operetta called *Die Fledermaus*, she appeared as herself. Two other justices, Stephen Breyer and Anthony Kennedy, also appeared with Ginsburg. All three wore their black justice robes and played party guests. Ginsburg dressed up her costume with a colorful fan. She has a reputation for accessorizing her judicial robes with fancy neckwear called jabots. A jabot is usually made of lace and hangs from the neck over a shirt or, in Ginsburg's case, over a Supreme Court justice robe.

For most of her life, Ginsburg was accompanied to concerts, operas, and other events by her devoted husband, Martin. He too had a distinguished career as an attorney. Later in his life, he was a professor at Georgetown University Law Center in Washington, DC. The Ginsburgs celebrated their fifty-sixth wedding anniversary shortly before Martin died in 2010.

Ruth Bader Ginsburg remains close to her children and her four grandchildren, though they live in different cities. Jane Ginsburg, the older of her children, is a law professor at Columbia University, the same school from which her famous mother earned her law degree in 1954 and later worked as a professor. James Ginsburg seems to share his mother's longtime love of music. He is a classical music producer in Chicago.

Along with being an inspiration to her children and countless other people around the world, Ginsburg is also a survivor. In 2014 she had heart surgery. After feeling some pain in her chest while exercising, she was rushed to a hospital in Washington, DC. Doctors placed a stent in an artery in her heart. A stent is a tiny, flexible mesh tube that helps restore blood flow in an artery that has narrowed. Ginsburg also had been treated for cancer in 1999 and 2009.

Despite these health challenges and her advancing age—she turned eighty-two on March 15, 2015—Ginsburg remains an energetic member of the Supreme Court, a guest speaker at university graduations and other events, and an involved grandmother. She also continues to exercise regularly.

ICON OF HISTORY AND POP CULTURE

Ruth Bader Ginsburg certainly has been a pioneer. When she started at Harvard Law, only about 3 percent of the students were women. In 2015 about half of Harvard's law students were women. As an attorney, she helped change laws that ended many types of discrimination, especially against women. And as a judge and later a Supreme Court justice, she continued to work toward a fairer society. "I try to teach through my opinions, through my speeches, how wrong it is to judge people on the basis of what they look like, color of their skin, whether they're men or women," she has said.

Ginsburg believes it's vital that women not be discouraged when they face adversity based on their gender. "Young women today have a great advantage, and it is that there are no more closed doors," the justice said in 2015. "That was basically what the '70s was all about. Opening doors that had been closed to women."

In 2015 Ginsburg received a medal from Harvard's Radcliffe Institute for Advanced Study. At the ceremony, Radcliffe dean Lizabeth Cohen noted Ginsburg's role in opening those doors: "We are here today to honor how one person—our honoree, Ruth Bader Ginsburg—knocked on closed doors, opened them, and held them open for others."

Cohen highlighted the justice's dedication to fair treatment for all. "What animates all her opinions is an unqualified commitment to fairness and a willingness to grapple with what the founders' vision of equality means today," she said.

At the end of the ceremony, Ginsburg was asked what advice she would give women today. "Fight for the things that you care about," she said. "But do it in a way that will lead others to join you." Certainly, a lifetime of fighting for fair play has

Ginsburg speaks to audience members during her medal ceremony at Harvard's Radcliffe Institute on May 29, 2015.

earned Ginsburg individual accolades and honors. But Ginsburg insists that she and the other justices place the importance of the Supreme Court above any personal goals or achievements.

Though the justices often disagree, Ginsburg said those disagreements never undermine the court itself. "We care about this institution more than our individual egos, and we are all devoted to keeping the Supreme Court in the place that it is—as a co-equal third branch of government, and I think a model for the world in the collegiality and independence of judges," she said in an interview.

While Ginsburg's legal career has cemented her place in American history, it has also made her something of a pop culture icon. In 2015 it was announced that actress Natalie Portman, who played Queen Amidala in the *Star Wars*

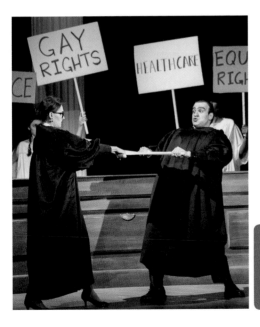

movies, would star in a film based on the life of Ginsburg. And in July 2015, a comic opera called *Scalia/Ginsburg* had its world premiere. The opera is based on the conflicting legal opinions and arguments between Scalia and Ginsburg.

Actors dressed as Ginsburg and Scalia perform in the opera *Scalia/Ginsburg* in July 2015.

Comedian Kate McKinnon performs as Ginsburg in a skit on *Saturday Night Live* in February 2015.

On NBC's *Saturday Night Live*, cast member Kate McKinnon made Ginsburg a recurring character starting in 2015. McKinnon would dress up in a robe and Ginsburg's trademark dark-rimmed glasses and pulled-back hair and make funny comments about her fellow justices and the news of the day.

There's even a Tumblr blog about the octogenarian justice called Notorious RBG. It's a reference to the late rapper and fellow Brooklyn native Notorious B.I.G. For her part, Ginsburg takes it all in stride. She has said she's amused by the attention and the number of people she meets who want a picture with her. Her grandchildren also keep Ginsburg updated with mentions about her in social media and mainstream entertainment.

But when asked how she'd like to be remembered, Ginsburg didn't mention the fame or all her accomplishments and all the barriers she helped knock down. Instead, in her usual humble manner, she said she hoped people would think of her as, "someone who used whatever talent she had to do her work to the very best of her ability. And to help repair tears in her society, to make things a little better through the use of whatever ability she has. To do something, as my colleague David Souter would say, outside myself. 'Cause I've gotten much more satisfaction for the things that I've done for which I was not paid."

While Ginsburg isn't one to boast about her amazing career, others are extremely quick to praise her. Back in the White House Rose Garden on that sunny afternoon in 1993, Clinton compared Ginsburg to former Supreme Court justice Thurgood Marshall, an icon in the civil rights movement.

"Many admirers of her work say that she is to the women's movement what former Supreme Court Justice Thurgood Marshall was to the movement for the rights of African Americans," Clinton said. "I can think of no greater compliment to bestow on an American lawyer."

Ginsburg *(center)* stands with fellow Supreme Court justices Sonia Sotomayor *(far left)* and Elena Kagan.

IMPORTANT DATES

1933   Ruth Bader Ginsburg is born on March 15 in Brooklyn, New York.

1954   She graduates first in her class from Cornell University in June. A few weeks later, she marries Martin Ginsburg.

1955   She gives birth to her first child, Jane, on July 21.

1956   She enrolls in Harvard Law School and eventually becomes the first woman on the *Harvard Law Review*.

1958   She transfers to Columbia Law School and serves on the *Columbia Law Review*.

1959   She earns her law degree from Columbia, finishing at the top of her class.

1963   She starts teaching at Rutgers Law School.

1965   She gives birth to her second child, James.

1972   She becomes codirector of the ACLU's Women's Rights Project. She also becomes the first woman to be a tenured professor at Columbia Law School.

1980	President Carter names Ginsburg to the US Court of Appeals in Washington, DC.
1993	President Clinton nominates Ginsburg to the Supreme Court. She is sworn in that fall.
1999	She is treated for cancer and recovers.
2007	Ginsburg writes the dissenting opinion in *Ledbetter v. Goodyear Tire & Rubber Co.*, which led Congress to enact the Lilly Ledbetter Fair Pay Act two years later.
2009	She receives treatment for cancer and recovers again.
2010	Her husband, Martin, dies soon after the Ginsburgs' fifty-sixth wedding anniversary.
2015	She celebrates her eighty-second birthday on March 15.

SOURCE NOTES

7   William J. Clinton, "Remarks Announcing the Nomination of Ruth Bader Ginsburg to Be a Supreme Court Associate Justice," *American Presidency Project*, June 14, 1993, http://www .presidency.ucsb.edu/ws/?pid=46684%20.

8   Ruth Bader Ginsburg, quoted in Richard Berke, "The Supreme Court: The Overview; Clinton Names Ruth Ginsburg, Advocate for Women, to Court," *New York Times*, June 15, 2015, http:// www.nytimes.com/1993/06/15/us/supreme-court-overview -clinton-names-ruth-ginsburg-advocate-for-women-court.html.

10   Ruth Bader Ginsburg, quoted in Nadine Epstein, "Ruth Bader Ginsburg: 'The Notorious RBG,'" *Moment*, May/June 2015, http://www.momentmag.com/ruth-bader-ginsburg-notorious -rbg-interview/.

12   Malvina Halberstam, "Ruth Bader Ginsburg," *Jewish Women's Archive*, March 1, 2009, http://jwa.org/encyclopedia/article /ginsburg-ruth-bader.

12   Ruth Bader Ginsburg, quoted in Sandra Pullman, "Tribute: The Legacy of Ruth Bader Ginsburg and WRP Staff," ACLU, accessed July 27, 2015, https://www.aclu.org/tribute-legacy-ruth-bader -ginsburg-and-wrp-staff.

19   "Ruth Bader Ginsburg: U.S. Supreme Court Justice," *Makers*, accessed August 19, 2015, http://www.makers.com/ruth-bader -ginsburg.

27   Ruth Bader Ginsburg, quoted in "A Conversation with Justice Ruth Bader Ginsburg," *Record* 56, no. 1 (Winter 2001), http:// www2.nycbar.org/Publications/record/winter01.1.pdf.

28–29   Antonin Scalia, quoted in Colleen Walsh, "Honoring Ruth Bader Ginsburg," *Harvard Gazette*, May 29, 2015, http://news.harvard .edu/gazette/story/2015/05/honoring-ruth-bader-ginsburg/.

29   Antonin Scalia, "Ruth Bader Ginsburg," *Time*, April 16, 2015, http://time.com/3823889/ruth-bader-ginsburg-2015-time-100/.

31   Ginsburg, quoted in "A Conversation with Justice Ruth Bader Ginsburg."

34   Ibid.

37   Ruth Bader Ginsburg, quoted in Irin Carmon, "Exclusive Justice Ruth Bader Ginsburg Interview," *MSNBC*, February 17, 2015, http://www.msnbc.com/msnbc/exclusive-justice-ruth-bader -ginsburg-interview-full-transcript.

37–38 Ruth Bader Ginsburg, quoted in Philip Marcelo, Associated Press, "Ginsburg Urges Young Women to Wage Inspiring Fights, available online at Radcliffe Institute for Advanced Study Harvard University, May 29, 2015, https://www.radcliffe.harvard .edu/news/in-news/ginsburg-urges-young-women-wage -inspiring-fights.

38   Lizabeth Cohen, quoted in Marcelo, "Ginsburg Urges Young Women."

38   Ibid.

38   Ginsburg, quoted in Walsh, "Honoring Ruth Bader Ginsburg."

39   Ruth Bader Ginsburg, quoted in "The Supreme Court," *C-SPAN*, October 4, 2009, http://www.c-span.org/series/?theSupremeCourt.

40–41 Ginsburg, quoted in Carmon, "Exclusive Ginsburg Interview."

41   Clinton, "Remarks Announcing the Nomination."

SELECTED BIBLIOGRAPHY

Burton, Danielle. "10 Things You Didn't Know about Ruth Bader Ginsburg." *U.S. News and World Report*, October 1, 2007. http:// www.usnews.com/news/national/articles/2007/10/01/10-things-you -didnt-know-about-ruth-bader-ginsburg.

Craig, Jon. "Ruth Bader Ginsburg Reminisces about Her Time on the Hill." *Cornell Chronicle*, September 22, 2014. http://www.news.cornell .edu/stories/2014/09/ruth-bader-ginsburg-reminisces-about-her-time -hill.

Halberstam, Malvina. "Ruth Bader Ginsburg." *Jewish Women's Archive*, March 1, 2009. http://jwa.org/encyclopedia/article/ginsburg-ruth -bader.

Pullman, Sandra. "Tribute: The Legacy of Ruth Bader Ginsburg and WRP Staff." ACLU. Accessed July 27, 2015. https://www.aclu.org/tribute -legacy-ruth-bader-ginsburg-and-wrp-staff.

Walsh, Colleen. "Honoring Ruth Bader Ginsburg." *Harvard Gazette*, May 29, 2015. http://news.harvard.edu/gazette/story/2015/05/honoring -ruth-bader-ginsburg/.

FURTHER READING

BOOKS

Haugen, Brenda. *Thurgood Marshall: Civil Rights Lawyer and Supreme Court Justice.* Minneapolis: Compass Point, 2007.
Learn more about the civil rights leader to whom President Clinton compared Ruth Bader Ginsburg.

McElroy, Lisa Tucker. *Sonia Sotomayor: First Hispanic U.S. Supreme Court Justice.* Minneapolis: Lerner Publications, 2010.
Read about Sonia Sotomayor, who grew up in a working-class family and eventually became a lawyer and Supreme Court justice.

Patrick, John J. *The Supreme Court of the United States: A Student Companion.* New York: Oxford University Press, 2006.
Get an A-to-Z guide to the Supreme Court's famous cases, justices, history, and current operations, as well as the definitions of dozens of legal terms.

WEBSITES

Congress for Kids: The Supreme Court
http://www.congressforkids.net/Judicialbranch_supremecourt.htm
Explore how the Supreme Court works and find out about famous cases the court has ruled on in the past.

The Interactive Constitution
http://constitutioncenter.org/interactive-constitution
Learn more about this key document of the United States, which Supreme Court justices work to uphold.

The Supreme Court
http://www.supremecourt.gov
At the official Supreme Court website, you can read about cases the justices are hearing and those that will soon go before the court. You can also read official opinions by the justices and learn more about the court.

INDEX